WHAT'S NEXT?

SURRENDERING YOUR PLANS TO JESUS

D1520817

FR. MIKE SCHMITZ

ASCENSION
West Chester, Pennsylvania

Nihil obstat: Rev. Richard K. McFadden
              Censor librorum
              June 6, 2023

Imprimatur: +Most Reverend Nelson J. Perez, DD
              Archbishop of Philadelphia
              June 12, 2023

Unless otherwise noted, Scripture passages are from the Revised Standard Version–Second Catholic Edition © 2006 by the Division of Christian Education of the National Council of the Churches of Christ in the United States of America. Used by permission. All rights reserved.

Ascension
PO Box 1990
West Chester, PA 19380
1-800-376-0520
ascensionpress.com

Cover design: James Kegley

Printed in the United States of America
23 24 25 26 27 5 4 3 2 1

ISBN 978-1-954882-20-1 (trade book)
ISBN 978-1-954882-21-8 (e-book)

CONTENTS

THE
SUNDAY HOMILIES
WITH
Fr. Mike Schmitz
COLLECTION

WELCOME TO **THE SUNDAY HOMILIES WITH FR. MIKE SCHMITZ COLLECTION**

Each booklet in this series has been created to invite Catholics to grow closer to God through reflections from Fr. Mike.

These booklets are short and relatable, with features that will help you apply what you read to your own life.

Quotes and Bible verses throughout the booklets will help you zero in on the key points.

Questions after each section prompt you to reflect and help you to dive deeper into the topic being presented. We recommend that you pray or journal with these questions as you make connections to your everyday life. (They also make great prompts for small group discussion, while keeping in mind that not everyone in your group may feel comfortable answering those of a more personal nature.)

Meditations are provided after each reflection to help you take the topic directly into prayer. We recommend setting aside some time after each chapter to read the meditation and pray or journal with it.

Each reflection ends with a challenge to put what you have learned into action. These challenges invite you to enter into prayer, serve others, make a resolution for the week, and more.

It is our sincere hope **The Sunday Homilies with Fr. Mike Schmitz Collection** helps you along the way in your journey toward holiness. May God bless you!

*Note: This booklet is adapted from a series of homilies given by Fr. Mike Schmitz.

CHAPTER 1

SOMETHING MORE THAN CONTROL

"What's next?" Isn't this a question all of us have?

Why is this? Because so many of us spend our lives in preparation for the next thing. That is almost what life is about, isn't it? It's about preparing for your next step.

A good parent prepares their children for what's next. Throughout the years, they get them ready for school each morning, which prepares them for what comes next. For most, this is earning a college degree or training in a trade, followed by a career.

We all need to prepare for what's next, which means we need to take some action. We need to get ready for what's coming next. The downside is that this can give us the idea or the notion that we have control over what's next. Preparation is good, because with preparation we can *influence* our future. But we cannot *control* our future.

It's safe to say that we all like a certain amount of control over our lives. But if we think about it for more than five seconds, we recognize that none of us really is in control. We might have the *illusion* of control, but we aren't *really* in control.

We might like things to be a certain way, but each of us is just a visit to the doctor and a diagnosis away from being out of control. When we are driving, we are just a traffic jam or an accident away from being out of control. In no part of our lives are we really in control.

> With preparation we can *influence* control,
> but we cannot control our future.

The moment the illusion of control disappears, usually suddenly, we can panic. At that moment, we realize, *I'm not in control!* We need to face questions like, "Can I be happy if not in control? Can I enjoy life if I don't know what's coming next?"

IT'S IN OUR DNA

Let's consider the early Church. The disciples just saw Jesus die and be raised, and now they are professing his message in a hostile environment. They have no power. They have no control. They have no political influence. Yet what do they do? As Acts tells us, "There was not any one needy among them, for as many as were possessors of lands or houses sold them, and brought the proceeds of what was sold and laid it at the apostles' feet; and distribution was made to each as any had need" (Acts 4:34–35).

They didn't sell things they didn't want or need. They sold their family homes, their family farms—the very things that gave them security, the things that helped them know what was coming next, the things that gave them a feeling of control. They sold them and gave the money to the apostles.

Imagine doing that now: selling your car, your house, everything you own, and then giving the money to your local bishop to do what he wants with it for the good of the Church. Doesn't that sound crazy? But that's what the first Christians did, and they seemed like they weren't even worried about it.

THE BELIEVERS SHARE THEIR POSSESSIONS

"There was not a needy person among them, for as many as were possessors of lands or houses sold them, and brought the proceeds of what was sold and laid it at the apostles' feet; and distribution was made to each as any had need" (Acts 4:24–35).

How can a person live like that? Did they do that because they were in control? Did they do that because they had power? Sometimes we can forget that the early Church was absolutely powerless. After all, the first several popes were all martyred, starting with St. Peter, the first pope.[1]

It wasn't until after the year 313, when the Roman emperor Constantine legalized Christianity, that a pope could actually live until his deathbed. Before then, Christians lived in profound uncertainty, and they seemed fine with it. Was it because they had control? No, because when we look at it, it is not in the DNA of the Christian to be in control. In fact, it is in our DNA to be rejected.

Think of the apostles in the Upper Room following Jesus' crucifixion. The doors are locked. They are mourning and fearful. Then Jesus appears to them, saying, "Peace be with you" (Acts 20:19). But what is the first thing Jesus does here? He shows them his hands. He is resurrected from the dead, but he shows them his wounds.

Jesus has conquered death, but he shows the apostles the nail marks in his hands and where the spear went through his side and pierced his heart. Then he says, "As the Father sent me, even so I send you" (see John 20:21). He is showing them what to expect.

So it is part of our DNA as Christians to expect to be rejected. This is one of the reasons why the Church needs something *more* than control. That's why *we* need something more than control. Every one of us needs something more than knowing what's next. We need what the apostle Thomas didn't have at first, and then got.

Remember, Thomas wasn't present when Jesus first appeared to the apostles in the Upper Room. When they tell him they have seen Jesus, Thomas replies, in effect, "No way. That didn't happen. I saw Jesus die. He is dead. I don't believe you." This is why we call him "doubting Thomas": "Unless I see in his hands the print of the nails, and place my finger in the mark of the nails, and place my hand in his side, I will not believe" (John 20:25).

Next week, everyone is there again, including Thomas. Jesus appears, and Thomas sees him. At the sight of Jesus, Thomas falls to his knees and says five powerful words—words that we say when we encounter Jesus in the Eucharist: "My Lord and my God" (John 20:28).

JESUS AND THOMAS

"Now Thomas, one of the Twelve, called the Twin, was not with them when Jesus came. So the other disciples told him, 'We have seen the Lord.' But he said to them, 'Unless I see in his hands the print of the

nails, and place my finger in the mark of the nails, and place my hand
in his side, I will not believe.' Eight days later, his disciples were again in
the house, and Thomas was with them. The doors were shut, but Jesus
came and stood among them, and said, 'Peace be with you.' Then he
said to Thomas, 'Put your finger here, and see my hands; and put out
your hand, and place it in my side; do not be faithless, but believing.'
Thomas answered him, 'My Lord and my God!' Jesus said to him, 'You
have believed because you have seen me. Blessed are those who have
not seen and yet believe'" (John 20:24–29).

Thomas now has something he didn't have before. He doesn't have
control. He has something more powerful than control. What Thomas
now has is *conviction*. From that moment on, he has no doubt whatsoever.
He knows Jesus has conquered death. He's convinced.

Thomas' experience helps us to understand why the early Christians
were able to sell their stuff and not be worried about the future. They
didn't worry about what would come next because they were *convinced*.
The word "convinced" comes from the Latin *con*, which means "with" and
vincere, which means "conquer." To be convinced means to conquer by
believing. Jesus Christ has conquered death. He has won the victory.

When I see the evidence, like Thomas, I am convinced. Jesus, who was
crucified, is now risen from the dead—and, all of a sudden, I am not
anxious about what's next. All of a sudden, I have a certain strength that
I didn't have before. Because I am convinced.

THEY WERE CONVINCED

Did you know that one out of every seven Christians throughout the
world faces high levels of persecution? And that over five thousand

Christians were killed for their Faith in 2022?[2] There still are martyrs, and these martyrs did not worry about what was next. They were convinced.

To be convinced means to conquer by believing.

Today, if you identify yourself as a believing and faithful Catholic, it can actually cost you in your relationships. Some might react to you along the lines of, "Oh, I get it. If you're Catholic, you're intolerant. You're judgmental. You're bigoted. You're homophobic. You're a hypocrite."

If you say, "I am Catholic," whoever you're talking to may label you with words that are not true. They may have it in their head that being Catholic means you are a "bigot," "homophobic," or "intolerant." For this reason, openly declaring your Faith might even cost you some future opportunities.

At the University of Minnesota Duluth (UMD), where I serve as campus minister, things are wide open. The university is generally very fair and accepting when it comes to establishing student groups, and every group is generally accepted by their peers—that is, until they take a stand and set some boundaries. Then, all of a sudden, tolerance gets tested.

For example, some students from the Newman Center started a new student group on campus called Bulldog Students for Life. They started hanging flyers that said, "We are a pro-life group." It took less than five minutes for those flyers to be torn down.

Now, there are a ton of different student groups at UMD, and everyone gets space. And everyone gets a sort of "stamp of approval." They put up their flyers, and some may think, *OK, that's a weird group*, but they have all been accepted … that is, until Bulldog Students for Life came along.

At one point, the group invited a nationally known speaker for an event called "Stump the Pro-Lifer." It was an opportunity for discussion and dialogue and an invitation for people who disagreed with the speaker's message to come and try to challenge her.

Guess what happened? Those flyers were defaced and torn down as well. Some even posted fake flyers with misinformation about who the Bulldog Students for Life were. In response, the pro-life group got some really tall people to post the flyers out of reach of the average student! The one poster I saw that wasn't torn down was plastered ten feet up with duct tape.

You see, the moment you take a stand is when, all of a sudden, people do not seem to like you as much. All of a sudden, it is no longer about being nice. It's about being *convinced*. It's about not knowing what comes next.

AN INVITATION TO SMILE

When someone doesn't like what we believe as Catholics, we don't have to get angry. Why? Because we are convinced. We remember that it is all about God's love and mercy. We don't have to get defensive because we are convinced that Jesus conquered death, and we have life in his name.

Right now, we can have life. We can rejoice. We can smile. My invitation to everyone this week is to smile. Now, you might say, "Father, how can we go from learning that thousands of Christians are killed each year … to smiling?"

Jesus conquered death, and we have life in his name.

Neither you nor I will probably be martyred for our Catholic Faith. Still, every one of us gets anxious at times when we think about what's next— whether that is tomorrow, next week, next month, or next year. So how can we look down the barrel of the next week, month, or year and smile? Because we are convinced that Jesus has conquered sin and death. He is in control.

We are convinced, and that is a reason to smile.

Right after Pope Benedict XVI was elected to the papacy, he stepped out onto the balcony at St. Peter's to give his blessing to the world. He looked like he was almost drowning in all the papal regalia he was wearing because he was a small guy, and it was a lot of robes. He had his arms up, looking out over tens of thousands of people in St. Peter's Square ... and he had a huge smile on his face.

We have always seen new popes come out like that—with huge smiles as they look out on the people. But when a cardinal is elected pope in the Sistine Chapel, he immediately goes to a room known as the Room of Tears to get vested in the white papal regalia. The new pope feels the weight of his new responsibilities. He realizes, *I'm not in control, Lord. You are. This job is bigger than me. I am not in control.*

How can the pope go from the Room of Tears to the balcony and have a huge smile? Because he is convinced. *Convinced.* Not that he was the best person for the job. If the Holy Spirit brought him here, he is convinced that God knows he is not going to wreck everything. He is convinced that the Lord brought him to this moment. And that is why he is able to walk out onto the balcony and smile. He knows he is not in control, but he is convinced.

So what about you? What's next?

Your future is uncertain, but you are *convinced*. Jesus is Lord. He has conquered death. God is the victor, and we all share in that victory that conquers the world, no matter what's next.

You have a reason to move forward in joy, rejoicing. No matter what's next, you have a reason to move forward with a smile, not because you are in *control* but because you are *convinced*.

What is something that you are looking forward to?

This question is not a judgment but a point of reflection: Would people describe you as a "control freak"? Would you describe yourself that way? If so, how does this tendency sometimes manifest itself?

How could the early Christians live with peace in the midst of such uncertainty? What would you need to be true in your life so that you would be able to face an uncertain future with joy?

Jesus showed the apostles the wounds in his hands and side and declared, "As the Father sent me, even so I send you." What are your thoughts about living as a Christian in a hostile world?

PRAY

Virtually everything in life is beyond your control. On any given day, you control virtually none of the circumstances around you. From the weather to the moods of those around you to your next heartbeat, you are not in control of the circumstances of daily life. Even your ability to enter into an unbroken, peaceful time of prayer is likely at the mercy of whether you are interrupted by something or someone.

However, as you enter into prayer today, ask the Holy Spirit to open your eyes to your supreme lack of control. Ask God to help you pay attention to everything you cannot control at this very second, starting with the breath you just took! As you breathe in and out, offer your breath to God in an act of gratitude, trust, and surrender.

Lastly, ask the Holy Spirit to replace your desire for control with a depth of conviction. In place of a need to control, allow God to give you absolute trust in him instead. Pray that you may be fully convinced of his sovereignty and of your powerlessness!

ACT ///

This week, do now what you know you need to do now.

CHAPTER 2

WHAT NOW?

If you could be anywhere in the world right now, where would you be? What would you be doing?

When I ask this question to groups, almost everybody responds: "I'd like to be *[somewhere else]* doing *[something else]*." Only about five percent reply, "Actually, I would like to be exactly where I am, doing what I am doing right now."

If 95 percent of the time, we would rather be somewhere else doing something else, what does that say about our hearts? What does that say about our lives?

One of the things it means is that we miss out on so much. If we would rather be somewhere else doing something else, we will miss out on many of the gifts that God and the people around us right now are offering.

If we would rather be somewhere else doing something else, we will be dissatisfied with our present situation. We will feel powerless and frustrated because we are not living right now but for another time, another place.

As we have talked about, many people are getting ready for what's next. If we live preoccupied with what's *next*, though, we miss out on what's *now*.

LIVING FOR NOW

Let's take a look at the Acts of the Apostles. Jesus has risen from the dead, and the apostles are convinced that he is who he says he is. Because of that, though, they don't have control; they have something more powerful than control. They are convinced that Jesus has conquered death. They are convinced, so they are no longer afraid of what's next.

In Acts, chapter two, we have Peter's first sermon on Pentecost Sunday. He proclaims that Jesus is Lord. He is the Messiah. Though they had crucified him, God raised him from the dead, and he reigns. "When they heard this, they were cut to the heart" (Acts 2:37). So they were convinced. Whenever Peter spoke with that boldness, with that power, they were convinced.

FROM CONVINCED TO CONVICTED

There is a difference between being *convinced* something is good for you and being *convicted* to do it. When we are convicted, we take action on what we know. Many of us have areas of our life like that. We are convinced that we should stop doing x, but we are not ready to do that— we are not yet *convicted* to make a change.

We are not yet "cut to the heart." But let's read on in Acts and see what happens: "When they heard this, they were cut to the heart, and they asked Peter the question, 'What must we do now?'" (see Acts 2:37). Notice that they didn't ask, "What's next?" They were convinced that Jesus had conquered death. They were convinced he is who he says he is. They were convicted, so they asked, "What must we do *now?*" Not later, but *now*.

Conviction always leads to action. I do what I have been convinced to do.

The recipe for being a boring Catholic is to be convinced but not willing to do anything with what we know. We might be willing to live for what's next, but we are not actually going to do anything now.

In Acts 2:38, Peter tells the people what they must do now: "Repent, and be baptized." Then he tells the people to repent and be converted (see Acts 3:19).

The original Greek word translated as "repent" here is *metanoia*, which means "a change of one's mind." *Metanoia* is also translated in the New Testament as "conversion." To be converted, then, means to change the way we think and act.

Metanoia (μετάνοια)—an ancient Greek word literally meaning "changing one's mind." In English versions of the New Testament, it is typically translated as "conversion."

Notice that Peter doesn't say, "Well, just go back home and try to be nicer to people." He doesn't say, "Well, just go home and say some prayers." He doesn't say, "Just be sure to pay your taxes." No, he says, "Be *changed*. Be *converted*."

HAVING A HEART LIKE JESUS

But what does it mean to be converted? It means having a heart like Jesus. It means having the character of Jesus. It means living like Jesus.

So when the people ask Peter, "What must we do now?," he tells them to be converted, to be changed, to be transformed. In other words, "Be like Jesus. Have a heart like his. Have a character like his."

How do we know we have converted? How do we know if we have changed? How do we know if we have a heart like Jesus? How can we be sure that we know him?

In his first letter, St. John tells us that the way we can be sure that we know Jesus and have a heart like his—the way we can be *certain* that we have a character like his—is to keep his commandments.

You may be thinking, "Yeah, I *knew* it. Catholics are all about the rules."

But it's about keeping God's commandments so that they form your heart. It is about doing the things you need to do now in a way that actually changes how you live.

Keep God's commandments so that they form your heart.

On January 15, 2009, US Airways flight 1549 took off from LaGuardia Airport in New York City. It was captained by a man named Chesley Sullenberger III. As it gained altitude over Manhattan, it struck a massive flock of geese, which took out both engines.

As captain of this large jet with no engines and 155 people on board over New York City, Sullenberger, known as Sully, had to make some quick decisions.

He couldn't go back to LaGuardia, and he couldn't make Teterboro Airport in New Jersey. There wasn't enough time. He couldn't land on a highway because of the traffic. So what does he do? He didn't consult the rule book. He didn't call someone and ask, "Hey, guys, here's the situation I'm in. What should I do?"

He made the decision to land on the Hudson River. With a dead stick, with no engines, with no power at all, he glided the massive plane to what they call "the miracle on the Hudson," saving every person on that flight.

Was he lucky? Maybe. But I think it's something more than luck. Sully had become a pilot when he was sixteen, and he flew almost every day. At the time of the accident, he had more than twenty thousand hours of commercial piloting—and had actually trained people in gliding.[3]

With all this training and experience, Sully knew what to do. He didn't need to consult a rule book. The rule book lived inside of him, so he knew exactly what to do. As he explains, " For forty-two years, I've been making small regular deposits in this bank of experience, education, training. And on January 15, the balance was sufficient so that I could make a very large withdrawal." He had spent decades of doing "what's now," and that prepared him for doing "what's next," even in the extraordinary situation his flight was in.

This message is for all of us. Living right now and doing what's now gets us ready for what's next. The Gospel of Luke tells us that Jesus said that everything written about him in the Law of Moses and the Prophets and the Psalms was true and must be fulfilled. Then the Gospel has this line that says, "He then opened their minds to understand the Scriptures" (Luke 24:35).

Jesus opened their minds to understand everything they had read in the past twenty or thirty years of their lives. We can only do this if we stop spending our time wishing we were somewhere else doing something else and actually pay attention to what's *now*.

This can be challenging to do, but the Lord is counting on you. To do what? To do what's now.

I know this is tough. Since I am the director of youth ministry for the Diocese of Duluth, I have monthly meetings with the bishop, along with all of the directors of the various diocesan ministries. Each of us has to give an update on what has been happening in our areas. This can be a tedious process. If no one else would notice, I would certainly have my laptop out, doing something else to pass the time. But I don't. I realize that the bishop is counting on me to be present and pay attention. That is my responsibility as a director.

The Lord says the same thing to you: "I'm counting on you to be here and to be now and to do what's now. The world is counting on you."

Think about all the time we have wasted, wishing we could be somewhere else doing something else, worried about what's next instead of doing what's now. Because we are *convinced*. We are *convicted*. All that is left is to be *converted*, to be *changed*.

The Lord is counting on you to do what's *now*.

But we run into obstacles that make it difficult for us to be changed. Questions start arising. People might challenge us, saying, "Is what you believe real? Is it really true? Is it really helping you?" And at some point, we might start doubting ourselves a little bit.

Let's use the example of a diet. This is not an endorsement for a certain way of eating or for dieting, and I'm not going to go into details, but the science behind this diet seems sound. I have talked to some people who are convinced it works and started following the diet for a few weeks. They said, "Yeah, it was hard at first because you basically have to give up certain foods, but then I started feeling better. I was more alert. I had more energy."

Now let's say you are on this diet and someone comes along and asks, "Hey, do you want a beer?" or "Hey, do you want a doughnut?" You would reply, "No, I'm on a diet." It is hard to say no, but you do. Because you are convinced, and you are convicted.

What if, though, after six weeks or so on this diet, you come across some articles that say the diet is not really the way, that it doesn't work long-term, or is actually unhealthy? Then some doubts get into your head. So the next time someone asks, "Hey, do you want a beer (or a doughnut)?," you think, *Well, why not? It probably won't matter this one time. Anyway, this diet might not even really work.*

You have the beer or doughnut, and pretty soon, you don't have the alertness you had. You no longer think clearly. You no longer have the energy you had. So you think, *OK, I guess this diet doesn't work after all.*

But maybe it wasn't the diet that didn't work. Maybe you didn't do what you needed to *make* it work. This can be what happens with so many of us when it comes to following Jesus.

We are convinced that Jesus is who he says he is, and we are convicted that we need to live like him. So we start living this way, but it is hard. But then I feel the Holy Spirit moving through me. I feel alive. I feel joy. Then someone challenges me: "But what about people who aren't Christians?" Good question.

"But what about all the suffering and evil in the world?" Another good question.

"What about prayers that aren't answered?" Yet another good question.

These good questions can become bad excuses for not following Jesus fully. I still think I am following Jesus fully, but actually I am cheating. Then I wonder why I'm not growing in my faith. This is what happens to so many of us. Nothing happens. We are not really changed.

NOTHING CHANGES UNLESS WE CHANGE

I love Alcoholics Anonymous (AA). I have seen the lives of many transformed by that group. One of the key sayings in AA is, *Half measures availed us nothing.*

This means that if you only half-heartedly try to be sober, you will remain an alcoholic. Similarly, if you half-heartedly try to be a Christian, you will not become like Jesus.

This is why I need to do what's *next.* I need to do what's *now.* But maybe I don't know what I'm supposed to do right now.

At the Ascension, Jesus says to his apostles, "And behold, I send the promise of my Father upon you; but stay in the city, until you are clothed with power from on high" (Luke 24:49). Then he ascends into heaven. Imagine them all standing there, saying, "OK, so what's next? How do we get the power from on high?"

What did they do? They did what they knew to do: They went back into the city. They paid him homage. They returned to Jerusalem with great joy. In fact, these are the last lines of the whole Gospel: "And they worshiped him, and returned to Jerusalem with great joy, and were continually in the temple blessing God" (Luke 24:52–53).

It is the same for us. If we are going to be fully converted in our hearts, we know we need to pray. If we are going to have hearts like God and a character like Jesus, we know we need to go to Mass.

But what if we fail at doing what's now? If we do the wrong thing, we have a defender in Jesus, who will show up and go to battle for us. Because we do not know what's next, but we do know what's *now*.

So how do you do it? You begin. You start with what's possible. You begin with what's now. You have absolutely nothing to fear about what's next.

REFLECT

If you could be anywhere in the world right now, where would you be? What would you be doing?

To be converted means to become like Jesus. We are like Christ when we live as he did. What are some obstacles to living like Jesus?

How do people who are convinced live differently?

Have you ever been distracted by naysayers or not know what to do? Discuss or journal about an example.

PRAY

Since you are here, you are likely convinced that Jesus Christ is the Son of God and Savior of the world. You may be convicted in your soul that there are changes in your life that need to be made to grow closer to him. But you must allow yourself to be converted, changed, and transformed—and that process starts now.

Instead of focusing on your past mistakes or hopes for the future, begin to allow the Holy Spirit to open your eyes to the life he has given you. Be willing to see the state of your life at this moment, and then be open to being ready for what comes next. Strive to live in the *now*.

Jesus clearly states that to live in the *now* and show that we love him, we must obey his commandments. Throughout the Gospels, Jesus commands his disciples to repent, take up their crosses, love one another, pray for their enemies, and preach the Good News, among other things. Each commandment of the Lord demands a decision from each of us *now*, at the present moment.

As you begin your time of prayer, ask the Lord to show you one thing that you can do *now* to help solidify your faith, trust, and love for him. Ask for the freedom to serve him and stay close to him. Remember that you are striving to keep God's commandments so that they form a way that changes how you live!

ACT ///

This week, make a practice of being attentive to the uncertainty and situations that disturb you … and remember that Christ has conquered. So smile in the face of the future.

CHAPTER 3

WHEN THE CHIPS ARE DOWN

Have you seen the film *A Quiet Place*? Before I went to see it, I read the positive reviews of it and completely forgot that it was going to be a scary movie. But it is not a *gory* scary movie, which I don't care for. I like movies that are about what they *don't* show you. That's the freaky part for me. The stuff that really gets under your skin is what you can't see.

In fact, one of the main characters in *A Quiet Place* is deaf. At certain times, the viewer is seeing things from her perspective—and hearing what she can hear, which is nothing. It is not knowing what's out there that is the scary part. I think this is why most of us were afraid of the dark as children. Or even as adults …

THE THINGS THAT SCARE US

People are afraid of the dark, not because the darkness is dangerous (unless you are walking through your house and run into the coffee table).

The thing that scares us about the dark is that we *don't know* what could be in it. It is our inability to see what's there that makes us uneasy.

I think the future is like the dark: what scares many of us is that we do not know what is in it. We can't see what will happen. It could be anything. So the main issue is that we don't know what's next. If we did, then we wouldn't be afraid. So we need something more powerful than fear.

We need to be convinced that Jesus is who he says he is. We need to be convicted so that we can live the Christian life. But we need courage to do this.

We hear a lot today about being fearless, right? On billboards, we see *Be fearless*. But that's a bunch of baloney. Courage is not a willingness to act in the *absence* of fear. Courage is a willingness to act *despite* our fear.

Maybe it is possible to be fearless when we don't need to do anything new. Maybe it is possible to be fearless if we never have to make a decision. Maybe it is possible to be fearless if we never have to be responsible for someone else. Maybe it is possible to be fearless if no one is counting on us, or if we take no risks. Then, yes, maybe it is possible to be fearless.

But that's not how we live. What do we do when the chips are down? What do we do when we are faced with a critical moment in our life, when we need to take a stand?

Courage is a willingness to act *despite* our fear.

The expression "when the chips are down" comes from poker. Think about placing your chips on the poker table. Until that moment, the game doesn't cost you anything. There is no risk. But the moment you put down your chips, you are taking a risk. You can lose. So you need to decide: Are you "in" or "out"?

COURAGE MAKES ALL THE DIFFERENCE

In the Acts of the Apostles, we read about an encounter Peter had with a disabled man while entering the Temple with John.

PETER HEALS A MAN AT THE TEMPLE

"Now Peter and John were going up to the temple at the hour of prayer, the ninth hour. And a man lame from birth was being carried, whom they laid daily at that gate of the temple which is called Beautiful to ask alms of those who entered the temple. Seeing Peter and John about to go into the temple, he asked for alms. And Peter directed his gaze at him, with John, and said, 'Look at us.' And he fixed his attention upon them, expecting to receive something from them. But Peter said, 'I have no silver and gold, but I give you what I have; in the name of Jesus Christ of Nazareth, walk.' And he took him by the right hand and raised him up; and immediately his feet and ankles were made strong. And leaping up he stood and walked and entered the temple with them, walking and leaping and praising God. And all the people saw him walking and praising God, and recognized him as the one who sat for alms at the Beautiful Gate of the temple; and they were filled with wonder and amazement at what had happened to him" (Acts 3:1–10).

A crowd was gathered around, astonished, asking, "How did you do this?" And Peter replies, in effect, "It's because of Jesus. You crucified him, but he raised you from the dead" (see Acts 3:11–16). And they were convicted to the heart. Then, members of the Sanhedrin, the council of Jewish elders, came and took Peter and John away.

The night that Jesus was betrayed, he was brought before the Sanhedrin. That same night, Peter was out in the courtyard, and he denied even knowing Jesus three times. This is the same scene. It is the same place, and it has the same people, the same cast of characters.

It is also the same danger, the same battle, the same risk. It is the same threat to Peter's life. But there's something different. And that something is Peter. In the current situation, the danger hasn't been taken away, but something has been given.

What's been given to him? As Acts tells us, "Peter, filled with the Holy Spirit, stood up and spoke" (Acts 4:8). What was given to Peter was the Holy Spirit—the same Spirit about whom St. Paul writes to Timothy: "You did not receive a spirit of cowardice that would shrink back in the face of fear. You received the spirit of power and of love and of self-control" (see 2 Timothy 1:7).

> "For God did not give us a spirit of timidity but a spirit of power and love and self-control."
>
> –2 Timothy 1:7

WE CAN LIVE IN THE SPIRIT OF COURAGE

The same Spirit that lives in St. Peter lives in you. God is not going to take away the danger. But he has given you the Spirit of power and of love and of self-control. He has given you the Spirit of courage. And all of us can exercise this courage.

Years ago, my friend Andrew was flying back home to California. At the time, he was in his early twenties and played guitar in a Christian band. He is an awesome guy, but he is not intimidating in his stature or appearance.

So on this flight, Andrew was seated next to the female CEO of a major corporation. Not surprisingly, this woman was super confident and polished, and she wanted to engage him in conversation. Since he is a friendly guy, he was happy to talk with her.

When he told her that he was flying home from a Catholic conference, her demeanor changed noticeably. As it turned out, she was a committed atheist. So their two-and-a-half-hour conversation was interesting, to say the least.

Now Andrew is really smart and well-versed in the Faith. So he could hold his own.

Knowing that these kinds of conversations can sometimes get heated, he has a technique to diffuse the tension. He says, "You know what? Isn't it just great that we get to sit here and talk about this like brother and sister? This is so great, isn't it? We can just love each other."

But this woman was not really listening to what he had to say, not taking it in. So Andrew prayed, "Lord, I think you want me to take this to the next level."

In the course of their conversation, this female CEO shared that she had an issue with her foot since childhood, something that caused her pain by just resting it on the ground. When she stood up and walked, the pain was excruciating. She had been examined by many doctors throughout her life, but she still had the problem.

As they were preparing to land, Andrew prayed, "OK, Lord, I've argued with her. What can you do now?" And Andrew looks at her and says, "You said your foot hurts a lot and no one's ever been able to heal it yet. Would you be willing to let me pray that Jesus heals your foot? And if he heals your foot, would you give your life to him?" He really said that.

And she looked at him and said, "Yeah, if he heals my foot, I'll give my life to him."

Andrew prayed, "Jesus, I know you love this woman, and she's suffering right now. Would you just show your glory? Would you be willing to heal her foot, to show her that you are real and that you love her?"

Almost immediately, the woman looked up and gave him a strange look, saying, "What did you just do? Something's happening to my foot! The pain is going away."

"OK, let's keep praying, then," Andrew said.

She said, "I'm freaking out. I don't feel anything. I don't feel any pain for the first time in my life." She looked at Andrew with wonder and said, "Jesus healed my foot."

Andrew said, "I know. Are you willing to give your life to him?"

"Absolutely," she said.

So he led her in a simple prayer: "Lord, I turn away from whatever it is you want me to turn away from. I turn my heart to you. I want to belong to you. I want to live for you for the rest of my life."

This healing was possible only because Andrew had the spirit of courage to share his story with her and engage her about his Faith. He was given exactly what he needed the moment he needed it.

THE RIGHT STUFF FOR THE RIGHT MOMENT

Courage is using what you have been given at the very moment when it is needed. It is using the right stuff at the right moment.

It is easy to be brave when there is nothing to be afraid of. It is easy to be honest when there are no consequences to telling the truth. It is easy to be prudent when you don't have any other choice. It is easy to be good when being good is easy.

In fact, C. S. Lewis says that courage is all the other virtues at the point when they are tested.[4] Courage is every virtue the moment that virtue is needed the most. If we do not have courage, we do not actually have any of the virtues.

When the chips are down, what do we do with what we have been given?

In John, chapter 10, Jesus makes a distinction between a hired shepherd and himself, the Good Shepherd. The hired shepherd clocks in on time and clocks out on time. He only hangs out with the sheep as long as he absolutely must. And when a wolf comes along, the hired shepherd runs away. The very moment the sheep need him the most—to fight for them and protect them—is the exact moment when the hired shepherd flees. Jesus, though, is the Good Shepherd. When we need him the most, he is there to fight for us.

SPIRITUAL BLINDNESS

"He who is a hireling and not a shepherd, whose own the sheep are not, sees the wolf coming and leaves the sheep and flees; and the wolf snatches them and scatters them. He flees because he is a hireling and cares nothing for the sheep. I am the good shepherd; I know my own and my own know me, as the Father knows me and I know the Father; and I lay down my life for the sheep" (John 10:12–15).

Look in your heart. In the last week, when have you needed Jesus to fight for you the most? Probably when you have been at your lowest, when you have failed. At that moment, when you need someone to fight for you the most, is when you need Jesus the Good Shepherd—because he loves you.

Remember, being convicted means more than just doing a couple of tasks. It means actually having the heart of Jesus, to have his character. This means that every one of us is called to have the spirit of Jesus, that spirit of courage.

HOW TO GROW IN COURAGE

How do we grow in courage? Courage is like a muscle or lung capacity. We make it stronger or increase our capacity for it by doing courageous things.

There is a movie called *The Rise of the Suffer Fest*. It is about obstacle-course racing. These are races where you dive into freezing water, get electrocuted, almost drown, and leap over fires. They are really painful.

In the film, they ask people who do those kinds of races why they do it. Most say that they do it because they want to grow. They want to be better than they are. Because if you have signed up for a race where you are going to get electrocuted and potentially drown, your response is, "OK, this scares me. It is going to hurt, but I can do it."

While we might never face the fear of participating in such a race, we probably do have an event coming up that makes us anxious. The night before, we will be thinking, "This scares me. This is going to hurt. But I can do this." We need courage, which is not the *absence* of fear but acting *despite* our fear.

We grow in courage by doing courageous things. I am sure you can think of some situations coming up in your life where you need courage. These do not have to be anything big. They can be simple. For example, maybe you have to give a presentation at work or school. Doing that presentation is you doing what you need to do when the chips are down.

Every one of us wants to get closer to Jesus. This is not a mystery. We all know what we need to do. We know that we need to pray. So we decide we are going to pray every day at 8 a.m. When that prayer time comes along, that is the moment of truth when the chips are down. That is the moment of courage. Even if you do not feel like praying, you do what you need to do.

How about when it comes to giving witness that Jesus is the Lord? Will you have the courage to do it when you need to?

I met a man a little while back who is a really intense Catholic working as a high-level executive at a big casino in Las Vegas. I asked, "How is it working there?"

He said, "I try to bring Jesus there."

"Yeah, but gambling destroys lives," I replied.

And he explained, "My job is to bring Jesus to every relationship I have."

Almost every day this man would interact with the president, CEO, and CFO—all the guys in charge of this big casino.

I asked, "How do you witness to them?"

And he replied, "I just bring Jesus into my normal conversations with them. For example, on Monday morning, when they ask me what I did over the weekend, I might say, 'We led a hundred kids on a retreat up in the mountains, and their lives were changed. It was incredible. It was really cool. Great weekend.' Or, I might say, 'We flew the family up to Montana for some skiing. On Sunday, we went to Mass, skied in the afternoon, and then flew back. It was awesome.'"

Now that is a simple witness. His coworkers came to know him as the guy who knows Jesus. When those other executives had a moment of crisis, they turned to him. A number of them were actually converted to the Catholic Faith due to his witness.

Courage is using *what you've been given* at the very moment that *what you've been given* is needed the most.

A CHALLENGE

This week, I invite you to enter into planned acts of courage. If you say you are going to pray now, then pray now. If you say you are going to meet your small group at a certain time, then meet them when you said you would. If someone asks you what you did this past weekend, tell them the truth and don't leave out going to Mass.

Plan acts of courage. Because to move to what's next, every one of us is going to need courage. To have the heart of Jesus when the chips are down, every one of us will need the courage that only comes from him.

REFLECT

What is one of the scariest things you have ever done? This can be anything from bungee jumping, to moving away from home, to speaking your mind in front of people who are intimidating. Please share or journal about this time.

Whenever we need to do something we have never done before, we need courage. Discuss a time in your faith when you had to act despite your fear.

Like Fr. Mike's friend on the plane, share an opportunity in your life when you felt called to give witness to your faith in Christ.

Without courage, it is not possible to live out any of the virtues. What is a virtue that requires more courage for you to live out?

PRAY

Isn't it amazing that we can know, love, and serve God and *still* be anxious when talking about him to others? There is often something daunting about the moment when we are on the verge of speaking about Jesus to someone, even though we are fully convinced that he is the world's Savior. We are so nervous that proclaiming his name might affect us negatively, aren't we?

As you begin your time of prayer, ask the Holy Spirit to bring to your mind a specific moment coming up this week when you will need the courage to speak his truth. Tell the Lord why you are nervous. Ask Him to help you have the courage to speak despite your fear.

Next, play out the scenario in your head. Allow God to guide your heart and thoughts to the right words to say. Remember that every person is searching for God, regardless of what it seems like on the surface. Everyone you meet is waiting for the light of God—his love—to shine into the darkest parts of their lives—and God wants *you* to spread his light.

Lastly, put yourself in the shoes of St. Peter. The first time he was challenged for being a follower of Jesus, he made a mess of the opportunity; he denied even knowing the Lord three times! After receiving the Holy Spirit, though, Peter courageously proclaimed the truth of Christ before the leaders of Israel in face of great opposition! You may have dropped the ball in the past and squandered opportunities to speak Jesus' name to someone who needed to hear it. Know that you are in good company with St. Peter. As you close out your time of prayer, ask for the intercession of St. Peter and make the intention that you will speak the name of the Lord with courage.

ACT ///

This week, schedule some planned acts of courage.

CHAPTER 4

GO *WITH*

There is a time, a season, when we have to go. We can't stay. In fact, much of life is like that. We have to move on. Even if we really want to stay, we have to go. What happens when we are at a time in our life when we have to go but want to stay?

We have already talked about what's next and wanting to have control, but that we need something more powerful than control. We need to be convinced that Jesus is who he says he is, and we also need to be convicted—we need to put our faith into action.

To do this, we need to take what we know, what we have been given, and use it in the moment when it is needed. We need courage. When we have to go, then, we need to be convinced, convicted, and courageous.

But we need something even more because, for a lot of us, it still comes back to control.

In 1999, a study was published in the *Journal of the American Medical Association* about people who were dying. People who *had* to go to what's next. They *had* to leave and had no choice about it. They were asked what was most important to them. As it turns out, the most valuable thing that these people who were dying wanted, but were losing, was a sense of being in control. Because when you know you are dying, little by little (or sometimes very quickly), every sense of control, every bit of it, is taken away.[5]

THE KEY IS CONFIDENCE

So when we have to go, how do we face it? How do we face losing that sense of control? The key is confidence.

Wouldn't it be amazing to be able to face what's next with confidence? Maybe you are already confident. You might say, "Seriously, Father, I don't know why you're hung up on this whole idea that the future is daunting or that what's next is scary. I'm not scared of anything."

If you're not afraid, maybe you have confidence because you have power or wisdom. You think, *I'm ready to go. Let me at it. Let me at 'em. I'll splat 'em.* (Remember that one? In *Scooby-Doo*, little Scrappy would say, "Let me at 'em, I'll splat 'em"?) Maybe that is you. You have power. You have answers.

What happens, though, when you are powerless? When you have no answers? How can you have confidence to face what's next?

BEYOND ANSWERS

I recently came across a story of a Filipino priest named Fr. Cirilo Nacorda. Fr. Nacorda was ordained in the early 1990s in the Philippines. His region of the Philippines frequently suffers terrorism from Islamic jihadists. Two years after his ordination, these jihadists stopped him in his car and took him captive, along with many other people who were driving on the same road.[6]

About half of the people that were stopped, about sixteen, were lined up along the road and shot.

When the jihadists discovered that Fr. Nacorda was a priest, they decided to hold him hostage and get the government to pay a ransom for his release.

But the Philippine officials refused, following the policy of most governments not to negotiate with terrorists. So the terrorists said, essentially, "OK, well, in that case, we will just behead you. This will show everyone that we are serious."

Fr. Nacorda was taken to a small hut, and chains were placed around his wrists and ankles, fastened together by a padlock. Four guards watched the building. As he says, "The night before I was going to die, I knelt down (which was difficult because of the chains) in front of these four guards and said, 'Jesus help me.'"

At that moment, Fr. Nacorda had a vision of Jesus. In the corner of the hut, a bright light began to grow. As his eyes focused, he realized, "I'm looking at the face of Jesus." He was so excited. He told the Lord what he needed, saying, "Jesus, save my life. Jesus, please set me free. Jesus, please get me out of here."

As Fr. Nacorda recounts, "Jesus was there, but he didn't say a word. He just smiled at me with the most beautiful face I have ever seen. And then he was gone." The chains didn't fall from his wrists. He didn't immediately have an answer. He still thought, "I'm going to die tomorrow."

But he didn't. For the next two months, every night Fr. Nacorda went to bed thinking that the following day he would be decapitated. And every night, he went to bed and slept like a baby. He had confidence.

Now, here is a man who was powerless, who had no answers. He didn't know what was next. How could he have confidence in this situation? He had confidence because he had surrendered his life completely to Jesus as Lord.

The word *confidence* comes from two Latin words: *con*, "with," and *fide*, "faith." So to have confidence is to live "with faith."

Many people have confidence because they live with faith. They live with faith in their strength. They live with faith in their ability. They live with faith in their intelligence. They live with faith in the hope that things will work out.

To have confidence is to live with faith.

What do the apostles have faith in? In themselves? In their own power? In their intelligence? In their own wisdom? Or do they have faith in something else? It seems clear from Scripture that they absolutely did not have confidence in themselves.

CONFIDENCE, NOT SELF-CONFIDENCE

Let's return to the story of Peter healing the man at the Temple. While walking into the Temple, Peter and John noticed a crippled man outside, begging for money. He looked up at them, thinking that they would give him some money. But Peter says, "I have no silver and gold, but I give you what I have; in the name of Jesus Christ of Nazareth, rise and walk" (Acts 3:6). Immediately, the man is healed, and he jumps up and down.

This event led to Peter preaching to the crowd that had assembled. He said, "Men of Israel, why do you wonder at this, or why do you stare at us, as though by our own power or piety we had made him walk?" (Acts 3:12). It was not their own holiness or strength that was able to make this man walk. He was healed in the name of—that is, through the power of—Jesus.

BY FAITH IN HIS NAME

"While [the man Peter had just healed] clung to Peter and John, all the people ran together to them in the portico called Solomon's, astounded. And when Peter saw it he addressed the people, 'Men of Israel, why do you wonder at this, or why do you stare at us, as though by our own power or piety we had made him walk? The God of Abraham and of Isaac and of Jacob, the God of our fathers, glorified his servant Jesus, whom you delivered up and denied in the presence of Pilate, when he had decided to release him. But you denied the Holy and Righteous One, and asked for a murderer to be granted to you, and killed the Author of life, whom God raised from the dead. To this we are witnesses. And his name, by faith in his name, has made this man strong whom you see and know; and the faith which is through Jesus has given the man this perfect health in the presence of you all'" (Acts 3:11–16).

When it comes to living holy, full, and joy-filled lives, how often do we think that we can do it on our own? But this is not possible with our own strength, with our own power. We can't have confidence in ourselves. We need to have confidence in Jesus ... in his power, in his strength, in his wisdom.

This is why John keeps repeating the words of Jesus in his Gospel: "Abide in me" (see John 5:4–10). So we have confidence in him.

JESUS IS ALWAYS WITH US

This is how we can both go *and* stay. We go, but we don't go alone. We go with Christ. To have confidence in Jesus is to *go with him.* As the Lord reminds us, "Apart from me you can do nothing" (John 15:5) Notice that Jesus did not say, "Without me, you can do *less.*" No, he said, "Apart from me you can do *nothing.*" We can't do some things "on our own," and some with Jesus. We have no power whatsoever without him.

A friend of mine is a priest in Virginia. He is not only the pastor of a parish but is also in charge of a Catholic high school. Some of his students started to make videos to communicate what they learned in their religion classes. One young woman, who plays the cello, gave an amazing example. Now, a cellist (or the violinist) can hold a note by drawing the bow back and forth smoothly across the string. This bowing creates a consistent, stable, steady note.

So this young lady made a video of her playing a sustained note on her cello, explaining, "As long as I keep playing the note, the music exists. But the moment I stop *[she removes her bow from the string]*, the music stops. This is how God creates the world."

Sometimes we can have the impression that God created the world, and then said, "OK, now go." As if creation were a one-and-done thing. But God is actively creating right now. Without God's active presence sustaining his creation, nothing would continue to exist—including you and me.

So when Jesus says, "Apart from me you can do nothing," he means *absolutely nothing.* To go back to our cello analogy, if God were to stop "playing" you, our music—our existence—would become silent. Think about that. We are his song, and he continues to play this music so that we continue to exist. "Apart from me you can do nothing."

How often do each of us try to live on our own, to do things apart from God? Jesus says, "Go with me," and we say, "Yeah, Jesus, I'll get back to you, but I'll take care of this first." This is the illusion of self-confidence, of self-reliance. We think we can do it on our own because we have power and smarts. We have the strength. We know we can take care of ourselves. But every time we fail, our confidence in ourselves fails.

When we are wrestling with a particular sin, we think, "OK, here's what I'm going to do. I'm going to take some steps. I'm going to do some things. I'm going take care of this myself." We rely on ourselves. Then we fail and only have ourselves to blame. So we get into a cycle of self-reliance, failure, and self-condemnation.

So how do we break the cycle? With surrender.

SURRENDERING TO JESUS

Why did Fr. Nacorda have such confidence as he was being held captive, facing execution? It wasn't because he had power. It wasn't because he had answers. It wasn't because he was counting on himself. He said, "I had confidence because I had surrendered my life to Jesus." If we want to remain in Jesus, we need to surrender our lives to him. If we want to have confidence, we need to surrender to Jesus.

Now, surrender is not quitting. Surrender is not giving up. Surrender is active. Surrender is actively placing ourselves under the lordship of Jesus.

What does it look like to surrender to Jesus? I used to think, *OK, Jesus, I surrender my life to you*, and then I would move on. I discovered that this is too general. I don't know what my life looks like if I just say that "I surrender." I needed to get specific.

So, for me, surrender means giving over specific events to him, especially what's next. The majority of my prayers are along the lines of, "Jesus, I don't know what's next. I'm going into this thing, and I'm going in blind. So I place this event under your dominion. I place it under your lordship."

When you are confused about the future, pray, "Jesus, I place this job search under your dominion." When you are in a difficult relationship, you might think, *I have no idea what God is going to do here. I have no idea how to get out of this relationship. I'm stuck. I don't know what's happening. It's tearing me apart.* So pray, "Jesus, I place this relationship under your dominion. I don't know what to do with it. So I place it under your lordship."

Maybe you are grieving the loss of someone close to you right now. So surrender, and have confidence in the midst of your grief to pray, "Jesus, I come before you in my grief. I'm placing it under your lordship. I place my grief and my broken heart, Lord, under your dominion."

> *Surrender* is actively placing ourselves under the lordship of Jesus.

Maybe you are entering a new phase in your life. Maybe you are getting married or having a baby. You think, *Wow, I'm going to be responsible to and for another human life. I don't know what to do.* Pray, "Lord, I place all of this under your dominion."

One of the reasons why so many people feel exhausted when they are facing what's next—when it comes to taking the next step—is because we are powerless and have no answers, but we try to hold on to our own power and answers. So we try to work our way through things. At first, this is fine.

Then what happens? Other things come up. We have new battles to fight. We are uncertain. We are afraid. What do we do then? We don't have to fight these new battles because we have already placed them under God's dominion. You might be sick, for example, but you have already placed yourself under God's dominion. Is the Lord going to heal you? He *might*, but you *know* you won't be alone. When you place a relationship under God's dominion, does that mean everything will work out? It might, but even if it doesn't, you won't be alone.

This is the most powerful response to "what's next?" Go, *but don't go alone.* Place everything under the dominion of Jesus. When we need to go, he will be going with us.

REFLECT

Who is the most confident person that you know? Where do you think their confidence comes from?

Share or journal about an area in your life where you were asked to go and how you felt in the moment.

We need to be convinced, convicted, and courageous—confident in Christ in moving forward. How can we do this?

Jesus said, "Apart from me you can do nothing." When it comes to living a full life, do you try to do everything in your own strength and power? How much do you rely on God and how much do you rely on yourself to do whatever task is in front of you?

When being encouraged to surrender something to Jesus, what thoughts and feelings come to mind at that moment? Do you mind it being a difficult thing to do? Do you find it an easy thing to do? Is there some uneasiness to it? Why or why not?

PRAY

It is normal to be anxious about challenges we are facing. As we have seen, virtually everything in life is beyond our control, so it makes sense to be a little nervous about certain possibilities. But what do we do with this anxiety about the future? The first step is to talk to God about it.

As you begin your time of prayer, ask the Holy Spirit to show you where you have placed your confidence for the future. Let the Lord show you where you may be relying on something other than him. Much of our anxiety about the unknown comes from knowing deep inside that we simply cannot control what comes next—and we are rushing into the future on our own.

As the Lord brings to your mind each instance when you have placed your confidence in yourself instead of him, offer him an act of surrender. Hand over all your anxieties to him. Pray, "Jesus, I place this under your dominion. I don't know what to do with it, so I place it under your lordship."

As you close your time of prayer, remember that you are in communion with the One who made every atom of the universe, each grain of sand on the seashore, and every soul in existence, including yours. You are not alone in this life. You are not heading into the future on your own—you are bringing God *with* you. Actually, God is in the lead, and you are following him! He is in the lead. So be at peace as you enjoy the wonderful gift of going *with* him!

ACT ///

What events in your life make you feel powerless? Bring them to prayer and confidently surrender them to the dominion of Jesus, knowing no matter what the outcome that you are not alone.

REMEMBER

- No matter what's next, there is a reason to move forward with a joyful smile—not because we are in control but because we are convinced that God is.

- We do not know what's next, but we do know what's *now*. So we start with what's possible. We begin with what's now. We have absolutely nothing to fear about what's next.

- To have the heart of Jesus when the chips are down, every one of us will need the courage that only comes from him.

- So what's next? We go, but *we don't go alone*—with go *with* someone. We place everything under the dominion of Jesus, and when we need to go, he will go with us.

NOTES

1   Fulton J. Sheen, *The Mystical Body of Christ* (New York: Sheed & Ward, 1935), 151.

2   These statistics come from the Open Doors study "World Watch List 2023." For more information, see Lisa Zengarini, "Over 360 Million Christians Suffering Persecution in the World," Vatican News, January 18, 2023, vaticannews.va.

3   See Captain Chesley B. "Sully" Sullenberger III's full biography at sullysullenberger.com.

4   C. S. Lewis, *The Screwtape Letters* (New York: Macmillan, 1946), 148.

5   Peter A. Singer, Douglas K. Martin, and Merrijoy Kelner, "Quality End-of-Life Care: Patients' Perspectives," *JAMA* 81, no. 2 (January 13, 1999): 163–168.

6   The story about and quotes from Fr. Cirilo Nacorda in this section have been paraphrased by the author. For the complete interview with Fr. Nacorda, see Tony Ganzer, "Facing Terror, Finding Hope: The Trials of Fr. Nacorda," *Faith Full Catholic Podcast*, April 14, 2018, faithfullpod.com.